SO-AIA-210

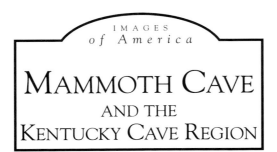

IMAGES
of America

MAMMOTH CAVE
AND THE
KENTUCKY CAVE REGION

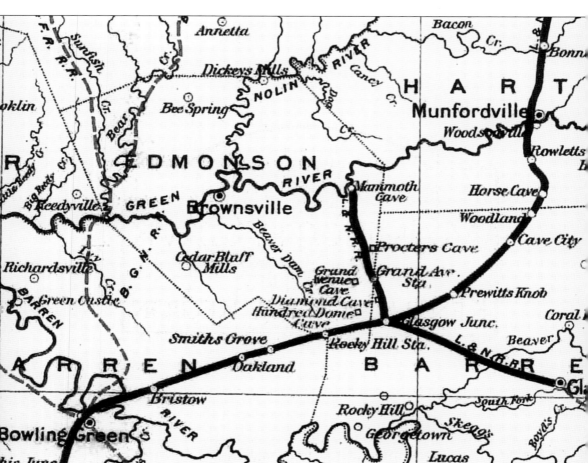

MAP OF THE MAMMOTH CAVE REGION, 1890. Mammoth Cave National Park and the Kentucky Cave Region are located in South Central Kentucky between Louisville and Nashville, Tennessee. The caves covered in this book are Mammoth Cave, New Entrance to Mammoth Cave, Great Onyx Cave, Floyd Collins' Crystal Cave, Sand Cave, Colossal Cave, Salts Cave, Ganter's Cave, White Cave, Dixon Cave, Dossey Domes Cavern, Procter's Cave, and Grand Avenue Cave. All are within the Mammoth Cave National Park. Hidden River Cave and Mammoth Onyx Cave (now Kentucky Caverns) are in the City of Horse Cave. Indian Cave and Collins' Onyx Cave are in Cave City. Diamond Caverns and American White Onyx Cave are in Park City (Glasgow Junction). Lost River Cave is in Bowling Green. The black line on the map from Glasgow Junction to Mammoth Cave represents the Mammoth Cave Railroad. Mammoth Cave, Diamond Cave, Grand Avenue Cave, Procter's Cave, and Hundred Dome Cave were the only caves exhibited to the public when this map was published in 1890.

IMAGES
of America

MAMMOTH CAVE
AND THE
KENTUCKY CAVE REGION

Bob and Judi Thompson

ARCADIA
PUBLISHING

Published by Arcadia Publishing
Charleston, South Carolina

Printed in the United States of America

Library of Congress Catalog Card Number: 2003100455

For all general information contact Arcadia Publishing at:
Telephone 843-853-2070
Fax 843-853-0044
E-mail sales@arcadiapublishing.com
For customer service and orders:
Toll-Free 1-888-313-2665

Visit us on the Internet at www.arcadiapublishing.com

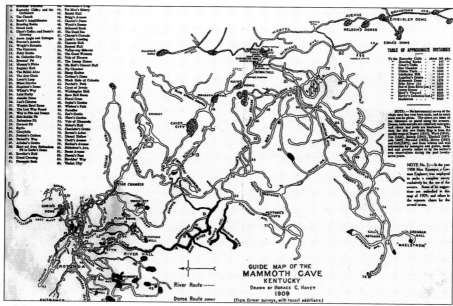

GUIDE MAP OF THE MAMMOTH CAVE, 1909. Numerous maps have been made of Mammoth Cave since 1811. Cave guide Stephen Bishop made a map in 1842 and it was published in an 1845 guidebook. Noted author Horace Carter Hovey made a cave map for his guidebook in 1882. Hovey also co-authored a guidebook with Richard Ellsworth Call on Mammoth Cave in 1897 that featured a map. Above is a map made in 1909 by Horace Hovey and included in his book *The Mammoth Cave of Kentucky, Illustrated,* published in 1912. It shows general direction but not an actual scale. This map became the standard reference map available to the guides and public for the next 50 years. The index on the left shows all the points of interest in the cave up to 1909.

CONTENTS

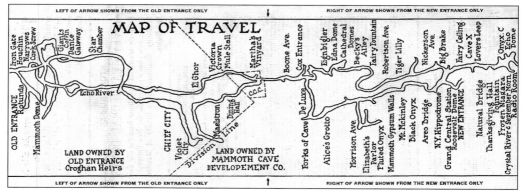

MAP OF TRAVEL, 1924. Mammoth Cave was once divided between two owners, the Croghan heirs (Old Entrance) and the Mammoth Cave Development Company (New and Frozen Niagara Entrances). This map shows the dividing line between the two cave owners between 1921 to 1931. The Kentucky National Park Commission purchased and took control of the New and Frozen Niagara Entrance in 1931, while the Mammoth Cave National Park Commission purchased the Old Entrance from the Croghan heirs in 1929. They both formed a joint operating committee in 1933 and held the property until it was accepted as a national park in 1941.

ACKNOWLEDGMENTS

There are many people responsible for the information found within these pages. The library staff at the Kentucky Library at Western Kentucky University in Bowling Green, Kentucky ranks among the best in supplying us with the finest sources of information on Mammoth Cave and the Kentucky Cave Region. For the past 10 years, it has been my primary choice when seeking information on the cave area. Other noted libraries include the Filson Historical Society in Louisville, Kentucky and the Ekstrom Library at the University of Louisville. Thanks to the staff at Mammoth Cave National Park who have inspired me since I was 11 years old with their first-class interpretation of the cave. Thanks to Mammoth Cave park ranger Charles DeCroix for the personal cave tours and for giving me a better understanding and appreciation of Mammoth Cave. Finally, a special thank you goes out to Mammoth Cave area historian Norman Warnell. If I ever had a question about Mammoth Cave, he always had an answer, and his knowledge of the cave area is truly remarkable.

INTRODUCTION

Mammoth Cave is one of the most outstanding cave systems in the world. The cave was one of America's first tourist attractions, preceded only by Niagara Falls. There is evidence that prehistoric people explored the cave 3,000 to 4,000 years ago. The remains of sandals, cane reed torches, and even a mummified body were found more than two miles into the cave. The cave was used for the manufacturing of gunpowder in the War of 1812. The long tradition of guiding underground tours at Mammoth Cave began in 1816. Under the direction of dependable guides such as the Bishops, the Bransfords, and others, an underground tour through Mammoth Cave was a memorable excursion. When Mammoth Cave became a national park in 1941, 40 miles of underground passages had been discovered and mapped since its initial discovery around 1797. Exploration at the cave has been continuous and new passages are still being discovered today. Other caves in the area were discovered to be connected to Mammoth Cave, and with over 350 miles of mapped passages, it is the longest cave in the world.

More has been written about Mammoth Cave than any other cave system in the world. Since the early 1800s, the cave has hosted a number of prominent writers, doctors, scientists, surveyors, preachers, poets, naturalists, and historians from around the world. There are many personal and detailed accounts of the cave, which were published in books, magazines, and newspapers. Some of the famous men and women who have visited Mammoth Cave are Jenny Lind, Ralph Waldo Emerson, Edwin Booth, Robert Montgomery Bird, Bayard Taylor, Nathaniel P. Willis, Helen Gould, John Muir, William Stump Forwood, Horace Carter Hovey, William Jennings Bryan, King Edward VII, Grand Duke Alexis, Dom Pedro II, Sir Julius Benedict, and William K. Vanderbilt.

Various photographers who were intrigued by the challenge of underground photography have taken pictures of Mammoth Cave since 1866. The earliest photographs were taken with magnesium (1866), flashpowder (1891), and flashbulbs (1931). Artificial lighting was limited and not easily accessible. It was only through trial and error that these early photographers could capture the full dimensions of the cave. Some of the famous photographers at Mammoth Cave include Adin Styles (1865), Charles Waldack (1866), Mandeville Thum (1876), W.F. Sesser (1886), Carlos Darnall (1889), Ben Hains (1889–1900), Frances Benjamin Johnston (1891), and Caufield and Shook (1931). These early photographers took many of the photographs used in this book.

The Mammoth Cave area was a key vacation site in the early part of the 20th century. Tourism increased with better transportation and the discovery of new caves. By 1930, at least 17 caves were either open or at one time had been exhibited to the public in Barren, Edmonson,

Hart, and Warren Counties. These included Mammoth Cave, New Entrance to Mammoth Cave, Great Onyx Cave, Floyd Collins' Crystal Cave, Colossal Cave, Salts Cave, Ganter's Cave, Dossey Domes Cavern, Grand Avenue Cave, Procter's Cave, Diamond Caverns, Mammoth Onyx Cave (now Kentucky Caverns), Hidden River Cave, Indian Cave, American White Onyx Cave, Collins' Onyx Cave, and Lost River Cave. Of all these, only Mammoth Cave (including New Entrance), Diamond Caverns, Kentucky Caverns, Hidden River Cave, and Lost River Cave give tours today.

This book shows in vintage photographs the history of the caves that make up the Mammoth Cave area from 1866 to 1941. Some captions include significant historical facts before 1866. Photographs are arranged as though the visitor is taking a trip to the cave area, beginning with their arrival and continuing with each cave. Vintage photographs, postcards, stereoviews, brochures, advertisements, and artist engravings are featured showing early transportation, hotel accommodations, cave guides (including noted African-American slaves), cave tours (souvenir photographs taken at the cave entrance), and the cave itself (including historic discoveries made in the cave).

We have selected the very best images from our collection for this book, and many of these photographs are rare and have never been published. They are a lasting tribute to the heritage of the Mammoth Cave region.

MAMMOTH CAVE AUSTRALIAN BALLOT POST CARD	Mammoth Cave, Ky._____191__	
The Cave is grand	The hotel is excellent	Let me hear from you
I made----------- ----trip	Meals abundant	Received no letter
I like Route 1	Lots chickens, eggs, milk	Received your letter
I like Route 2	No cold storage meats	Don't worry
I like Route 3	Water perfectly pure	You're always in my mind
I like Route 4	Rate only $2.00 per day	Don't forget me
Rate: One route, $2.00	Grounds are beautiful	With best regards
Additional route, $1.00	Am feeling fine	Good-bye for the present
--------is a good guide	Will remain ------days	Remember me to--------
Cave temp. always 54°	May come here again	My love to -------------
Air pure. No germs	About---people here now	Love to the kids
Great place for health	I leave here-----------	Having time of my life

LINES CROSSED BEAR MY SENTIMENTS

AUSTRALIAN BALLOT POSTCARD, C. 1910. A postcard with a pre-printed message was an easy way for early cave visitors to express themselves to friends at home. The postcard contains 36 phrases in boxes in which the sender marked items with an "X" that shared his sentiments.

One

MAMMOTH CAVE

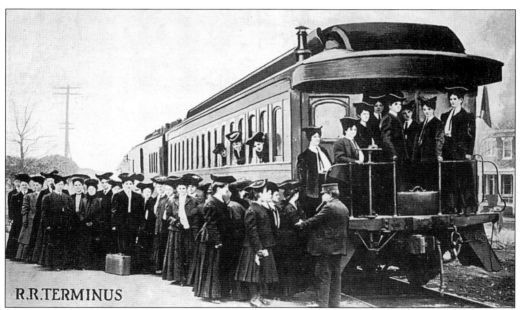

A TRIP TO MAMMOTH CAVE, C. 1908. The L&N Railroad started passenger rail service between Louisville and Nashville on October 31, 1859. Two main stops were at Cave City and Glasgow Junction, which is known today as Park City. Here a school party boards the train at Glasgow Junction. The Mentz Hotel can be seen on the right.

L. and N. R. R. Depot, Glasgow Junction, Ky.

Mammoth Cave R. R. Dummy Train, Glasgow Junction, Ky.

GLASGOW JUNCTION, C. 1914. The L&N Railroad brought passengers within 10 miles of Mammoth Cave in 1859. From there they traveled by stagecoach to the cave. The top photograph shows the arrival of the L&N train at the Glasgow Junction Depot. Tourists started traveling on the Mammoth Cave Railroad Dummy Train (bottom) from the depot to the cave in 1886.

BELL TAVERN, 1908. Bell's Tavern was across the road from the Glasgow Junction Depot, and just to the right of the Mentz Hotel. Built in the 1820s, this famous old inn served as a resting place for travelers to Mammoth Cave up until the Civil War. Work began in 1860 to update the exterior and interior in order to make the inn a world-class establishment. Unfortunately, work stopped when the Civil War began, and never resumed. Only the remains of the tavern can be seen today.

THE MENTZ HOTEL, 1905 AND 1908. The Mentz Hotel was directly across from the Glasgow Junction Depot. If it was too late in the day to catch a train to Mammoth Cave, guests would often spend the night here. C.H. Smith of Bowling Green built the hotel in 1885. E.H. Mentz purchased it from Schuler Renfro in 1905. The photograph above, entitled "The New Mentz Hotel," was taken soon after Mentz's purchase. E.H. Mentz is seen in the 1908 photograph below; he is standing in front of the hotel, outside the gate. After Mentz, Hade Burnett and Mrs. O.H. Fishback operated the hotel. In 1946, the building was run as a boarding school for boys. The building was also an apartment house in 1954, and a nursing home between 1955 and 1966. Today the hotel is a private residence.

3272 – Mentz Hotel, Glasgow Junction, Ky.

THE DINKEY TRAIN, 1906. An 8.7-mile railroad extension was completed from the Glasgow Junction Depot to the Mammoth Cave Hotel in 1886. Stops were made between the depot and cave at Diamond Caverns, Grand Avenue Cave (on a branch line), Chaumont Post Office, Union City, Procter's Hotel, Sloan's Crossing, and Ganter's Hotel.

MAMMOTH CAVE DINKEY, C. 1910. The first passenger to ride on the Mammoth Cave Railroad was a man named W.F. Richardson on November 8, 1886 (ticket no. 1350) at a cost of $3. Besides passengers, the Mammoth Cave Railroad carried food and supplies to the hotel at the cave and had a contract to carry United States mail.

The Dinkey Train u Mammoth Cave Ky

THE DINKEY TRAIN, 1909. The Mammoth Cave Railroad purchased four secondhand dummy-type Baldwin locomotives for use on its railroad line. A dummy engine is a locomotive with condensing engines, and therefore it operates without the noise of escaping steam. An advantage of the quieter engine was that it did not scare the horses. The "Hercules" (#3) claimed the greatest fame among the four locomotives. The train carried a three-man crew that included the engineer, conductor, and fireman. One of the best-known engineers was Pat Moran (in front). Robert Hatcher (in rear) was one of the best-known conductors. The handwritten message on the back of this postcard reads, "This is the train Papa and I rode on up to the cave yesterday only it had two more cars on it. We went about as fast as you could drive with an old horse and buggy."

MAMMOTH CAVE TRAIN, C. 1905. This was not one of the better days for the train, as there is only one passenger for at least seven railroad employees. Notice the water tank in the photograph. Water tanks were necessary for the steam engines and were located at Glasgow Junction and at Mammoth Cave.

MAMMOTH CAVE TRAIN, C. 1920. The Mammoth Cave Train could carry as many as 200 guests per trip. Because of the way the railroad was built, top speed for the train was only 35 mph. The last steam-driven locomotive traveled over the Mammoth Cave Railroad in the 1920s and was replaced by a railbus until September 1, 1931, when service was discontinued. Engine #4, shown above, made the last trip in the fall of 1931 and can be seen today at Mammoth Cave National Park.

L&N Railroad Advertisement, 1913. This four-page L&N advertising flyer called Mammoth Cave "The greatest wonder of the world." It promoted a weekend excursion trip to Mammoth Cave from Cincinnati, Ohio on July 12, 1913, declaring, "Our patrons who availed themselves of our Excursions say that one does not realize the train service, attention shown on these popular weekend trips, until one visits Mammoth Cave. The compliments we receive are numerous. Every little detail is looked after from the beginning until we return. It is a continuous round of pleasure. There is no other trip that offers so much for the time and small expenditure as this picturesque excursion to the Wealth of an Under World Scenery." The cost of the entire trip, including railroad fare, cave fees, hotel, and meals, was $11.75.

ARCH ENTRANCE, C. 1920 AND C. 1930. The arch entrance to the Mammoth Cave hotel and grounds is shown here before it became a national park. Tourists were warned in a 1920s brochure (featuring the above photograph), "Do not stop or turn off the road until this archway is reached, 11 miles from Cave City," to keep them from being intercepted by competing caves. The building on the right in the 1930s photograph below is the Demunbrun Store. The store was an integral part of visitor activity at Mammoth Cave. It served as a grocery store, post office, and souvenir shop. The building was torn down in 1939. Notice the competitor's signs for Great Onyx Cave and Floyd Collins' Crystal Cave.

MAMMOTH CAVE RAILROAD, C. 1918. The Mammoth Cave Railroad ended just beyond the Demunbrun Store shown on the right. From here, guests would walk a short footpath to the Mammoth Cave Hotel.

MAMMOTH CAVE ROUTE, C. 1905. The building of locks and dams on the Green River brought steamboats and towboats from Bowling Green and Evansville to the cave. The Evansville & Bowling Green Packet Company had an "All River Excursion Route to Mammoth Cave" during the summer months on the steamboat *Chaperon*.

17

THE BOAT LEONA, JULY 27, 1907. The Myers Packet Company also had an excursion route to the cave. Here a party arrives on the boat *Leona* at the Mammoth Cave Landing, which was just below the Historic Entrance to the cave.

ON GREEN RIVER, 1908. The wooden boat structure is the Mississippi War Museum, which was loaded with Civil War relics and other mementos. The historic *Hobson*, as it was called, was educational and owned by Captain Berry. It was docked at the ferry landing at Mammoth Cave.

"In ye olden time."

STAGECOACHES, 1896. The earliest stagecoach line to Mammoth Cave was from Glasgow Junction at Bell's Tavern. In the summer of 1833, J.H. Harlow drove the first stagecoach to Mammoth Cave. Later, Andy McCoy operated a stage line from Cave City to Mammoth Cave with two coaches named the "Florida" and the "John E. Bell." Upon arrival at the Mammoth Cave Hotel, the sound of a bugle would herald the arrival of the stage. This would alert the hotel manager and servants who stood ready to offer their services to the guests.

AUTOMOBILE AT MAMMOTH CAVE HOTEL, C. 1910. The first automobile arrived at Mammoth Cave on October 7, 1904, and was reportedly driven by a judge from Indianapolis, Indiana. The event was memorable from the moment the judge and his chauffeur came to a clattering stop at the arch entrance and became stuck in the mud. The manager of the hotel brought out a pair of mules and pulled the car out of the mud hole. The occupants of this car from that early era are unknown.

HOTEL YARD, 1889. The Mammoth Cave Hotel originally started as log cabins that were built and used by saltpeter miners around 1812. The cabins formed the core of the building, and were later connected and weatherboarded under the cave ownership of Franklin Gorin from 1837 to 1839. The top photograph is a view of the hotel yard, looking southwest at the connected cabins. The bottom photograph shows the view to the south.

HOTEL, MAMMOTH CAVE, C. 1905. Mammoth Cave Hotel was considered one of the finest hotels in the state. John Croghan owned the hotel and cave from 1839 to 1849 and constructed the large two-story building that included a first-floor dining room and a second-floor ballroom.

MAMMOTH CAVE HOTEL, 1915. A veranda was added to the front of the Mammoth Cave Hotel during the 1910s. There was a bandstand to the right of the veranda (not shown). Music was often played here to welcome guests as they arrived at the hotel. A string band played at the hotel each summer, with music at meal times and at dances at night in the large ballroom.

MAMMOTH CAVE HOTEL, 1908. Mammoth Cave was a vacation destination for many guests. They came not only to see the famous cave, but also to relax. The ballroom at the hotel was one of the most enjoyable places to spend an evening. Guests sat and talked around the great log fires, or danced to the music of orchestras. Hotel rates in 1908 ranged from $2.50 to $3 per day for the new bungalow, with bath. These prices included meals.

MAIN HALL, 1889. In the large hallway going into the hotel, curio venders displayed stalactites, baskets, pipes, shells, and pictures. At the far end of the hall was the photographer's office where photographs of cave parties were displayed. The dining room was located on the ground floor and the ballroom was upstairs. The hotel dining room had a long table, which seated 300.

MAMMOTH CAVE HOTEL, C. 1930. In 1925, a new hotel replaced the old one that burned to the ground on December 9, 1916. An addition was built in 1930. The new hotel provided sleeping accommodations for 200 visitors, and the dining room seated 125 guests at one time. In 1979, the hotel no longer met safety regulations and was demolished after the present hotel at Mammoth Cave was completed in 1965.

MAMMOTH CAVE HOTEL, C. 1930. The hotel was the starting point for four of the six cave tours that were offered in the 1930s. The two other tours started at the New Entrance Hotel.

MR. GRAVES AND OUR PARTY, 1871. David L. Graves (third from the left) was manager of the Mammoth Cave Hotel and agent for the cave from 1871 to 1874. He was also proprietor of the Cave City Hotel and ran a stage line that competed with the one run by Andy McCoy. Mammoth Cave had many hotel managers during its lifetime. After owner John Croghan died in 1849, he requested in his will to rent out the lands and buildings (except the cave) for five-year terms. Some of the hotel lessees include William S. Miller Sr. (1850–1856 and 1875–1881), Larkin J. Procter (1856–1861 and 1866–1871), E.K. Owsley (1861–1866), David L. Graves (1871–1874), Francis Klett (1881–1883), William Charley Comstock (1883–1888), Henry C. Ganter (1888–1902), and Willis W. Renshaw (1902–1911). In this engraving, Graves is shown socializing with a new arrival of hotel visitors. Guide William Garvin is second from the left.

COMSTOCK'S KITCHEN CABINET, 1887. Charley Comstock was manager of the Mammoth Cave Hotel from 1883 to 1888. Comstock had many years of experience in the hotel business. Along with his wife, brother, and nephew, Comstock managed the hotel in an "efficient and pleasant manner as to please the public," according to an old guidebook on the cave. He advertised the hotel and cave extensively. The Mammoth Cave Railroad opened in 1886 while he was proprietor of the cave hotel. Adjoining Comstock's office was a display case where cave specimens were for sale. Formations were not to be taken from the cave. To prevent anyone from finding a new entrance, another rule prohibited the use of surveyor's instruments in the cave. Comstock is shown seated in this photograph outside the hotel with his kitchen help. The kitchen crew slaughtered their own cows, hogs, and chickens, and had fresh milk and eggs every day as well.

01 ½ The Entrance looking down, Mammoth Cave.

HENRY C. GANTER, C. 1900. Henry C. Ganter (1844–1917) was manager of Mammoth Cave Hotel between 1888 and 1902. During some of this time he was also agent for the cave. Ganter made many improvements to the old hotel and grounds. According to a newspaper article, he remodeled many of the hotel rooms as well as the dining room, which included a "three-story kitchen with elevator and dumb waiters to cut off all unnecessary help." Ganter also added a specimen room and a bar for the visitors. He was known to entertain visitors for hours at the hotel with his knowledge of the cave. Ganter's obituary from 1917 states that he spent a total of 25 years managing, which was more than any other manager at Mammoth Cave. After Mammoth Cave, he opened his own hotel, "Ganter's Hotel," which was located on the Mammoth Cave Railroad line. This photograph shows Ganter at the entrance looking down into the cave.

GUIDE, STEPHEN BISHOP. One of the earliest (1838) and most famous of all Mammoth Cave guides was a slave named Stephen Bishop. He had more to do with the early exploration of Mammoth Cave than any other guide and was described in books as self-educated, informative, and charming. Stephen came in contact with both the casual visitor as well as prominent scientists. He guided the singer Jenny Lind; Ole Bull, the Norwegian violinist; and poet Ralph Waldo Emerson.

STEPHEN BISHOP GRAVE. Stephen Bishop died in 1857 and is buried in the cemetery near the Historic Entrance to Mammoth Cave. A grave marker was erected at Stephen's grave in 1881, 24 years after he died. The inscription read, "Stephen Bishop, First Guide & Explorer of the Mammoth Cave, Died June 15, 1859 in his 37 year." Note the incorrect year of his death.

GUIDES, MAT AND NICK, 1865. Mat and Nick Bransford were also two well-known slave cave guides at Mammoth Cave. They were not brothers, but took the last name of their former owner, Thomas Bransford. They were leased to cave owner Franklin Gorin in 1838. Mat and Nick started leading tours in 1838 and mastered the art of guiding with their knowledge of the cave. Mat assisted Charles Waldack, a photographer, in taking the first underground photographs of the cave in 1866. He also helped discover "Mammoth Dome" and "Serena's Arbor." Nick helped discover "Stevenson's Lost River" in 1863 and took part in the descent into the "Maelstrom" pit. Both Mat and Nick saved a party from drowning in Echo River. Mat died in 1886, and Nick died in 1894. This photograph shows Mat and Nick sitting in front of the natural entrance to the cave.

GUIDE, WILLIAM GARVIN, 1891. William Garvin (c. 1853–c. 1910) guided at the cave between 1861 and 1902. William was credited in 1870 for the discovery of "The Corkscrew," a narrow passage used until the Mammoth Dome Tower steel stairway was completed in 1957. He discovered the Corkscrew after deductions he made by observing the movements of bats in the cave. Will also discovered "Martha Washington's Statue," one of the beautiful illusions of Mammoth Cave in 1882. After Stephen Bishop died in 1857, his wife Charlotte later married William Garvin. There is a passageway in the cave named for him, "Wm Garvin's Way." The famous woman photographer Frances Benjamin Johnston took this photograph of William during her visit to the cave in 1891. According to Johnston, "All through my siege of the black depths with photographic battery and flash-powder, William was my most trusted ally, and aided very materially in the ultimate success of the venture."

WILLIAM GARVIN, C. 1909. The most striking accomplishment of William Garvin was his good humor. He possessed an endless array of jokes and puns and was clever and funny enough to raise a laugh with guests every time. William used to cap his jokes by jumping high and clicking his heels together twice before landing on his feet again. Once he jumped so high he bumped his head on the cave ceiling and knocked himself out. All of the cave guides lived near the cave. Even though they lived a simple life, they were much respected by visitors for their knowledge. This is a photograph of William shortly before he died.

GUIDE, WILLIAM BRANSFORD, C. 1900. A second generation of the Bransford family, Henry (1849–1894), the son of Mat, guided at the cave between 1875 and 1894. William (1866–1934) (above) was the nephew of Mat and guided between 1888 and 1932. Both Henry and William inherited qualities that made them exceptional guides. William helped discover the part of the cave known as "Cathedral Domes" in 1907. He was described in books as "a tall, spare, wiry man, full of information not only of the cave, but also of subjects that cave lore suggests." There is a passageway in the cave named for him called "Bransford Avenue." Henry died in 1894 and William died in 1934. Guide Ed Bishop is in the background.

BISHOP THE GUIDE, 1905. Cave guides often gave guests a picture-postcard of themselves as a souvenir of their tour. Many of the postcards can be found with signatures and other notes of interest. For example, this card was inscribed on the back (shown below) by guide Ed Bishop ("Bishop the Guide, been guide since 1887."). Early tourists sometimes wrote notes about their guide, including the following found on this card: "Bishop the Guide (a mulatto) gave this picture to Forrest C. Respess in 1905, was guide of our party. He and his family lived in a cabin near the cave. His father had explored and guided for many years before he was old enough to explore."

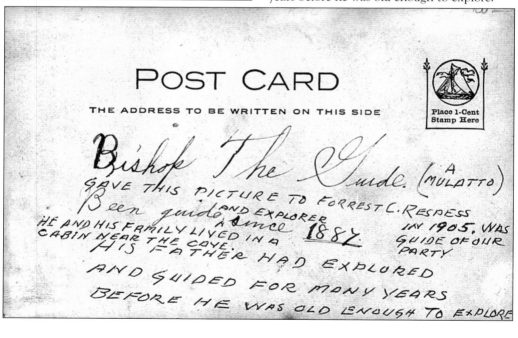

YOURS TRULY, BISHOP THE GUIDE, 1905. Ed Bishop (1866–1932), a descendant of the famous Mammoth Cave guide Stephen Bishop, guided tours from 1887 until 1917. Ed, accompanied by Max Kämper, a surveyor from Germany, discovered "Violet City" in 1908 by finding a way through "Ultima Thule," which was considered the end of the cave at that time. Ed assisted Kämper for eight months as Kämper made a new map of the cave. The map was considered very accurate but was kept under lock and key for many years because it showed passages going beyond the Mammoth Cave Estate. There is a place in the cave named after Ed known as "Bishop's Pit." On this card, Bishop signed "Yours Truly" and his name in reverse on the negative before the postcard was printed, resulting in several backwards letters. Ed Bishop died in 1932.

JOSHUA WILSON, GUIDE, 1905. Owen Joshua Wilson (1857–1928) (or "Josh," as many knew him) guided at the cave between 1884 and 1924. Once known as the "Dean of Guide Corps" in the 1920s, Josh took this honor lightly, and his humorous philosophy soothed many a visitor to the cave. At one time, Josh also drove the stagecoach from Cave City to the cave. There is a cave passage named after Josh known as "Wilson's Way." Notice in this photograph the hand-held, open-flame lard oil lamps that were used to illuminate early cave tours. In addition to these, each guide carried an extra supply of lard oil, a bag of Bengal lights (flares also used to light the cave), and twisted oiled rags (also used for illumination purposes). Modern-day cavers continue the practice of carrying at least three sources of light before exploring any cave.

YOURS TRULY, JOSH WILSON, 1908.
According to locals of the cave region, caving gets into the blood. This is evident by the fact that many cave guides were the sons and grandsons of guides. It has become a tradition for the children of guides to follow the professions of their fathers, and they are proud of their heritage and their cave. Josh had two sons that followed him in this tradition, Cebert and Lloyd. They started guiding at Mammoth Cave around 1918. Cebert guided until 1965.

GUIDE, ROBERT LIVELY, 1905. Bob Lively (1867–1940) was a full-time cave guide between 1890 and 1915. He continued to give occasional tours until the 1930s. In addition to his guide duties, Bob was also involved in the early exploration of nearby Colossal Cave. There is a place in Mammoth Cave named after Bob known as "Lively's Pass." Early guides at Mammoth Cave were known to be courageous, resourceful, and ready for any emergency that might arise during the performance of their jobs. Each guide knew the exact number of visitors they brought into the cave, and as they counted their party frequently, the rescue of a stray visitor seldom took more than a few minutes. The responsibility of guiding visitors through the caves, generation after generation, has built a deep sense of duty within guides.

John M. Nelson, Guide, M.C., Ky.

This represents "our" good guide Grace Hath away

Sept. 4, '05.

GUIDE, JOHN NELSON, 1905. John M. Nelson (1867–1956) of Glasgow was a guide at Mammoth Cave between 1894 and 1905. It was said that he made as many as 4,540 trips in the cave and exhibited it to 31,807 different people. Nelson guided Horace Carter Hovey, the noted researcher, writer, and lecturer on caves. Although Nelson quit guiding and started a painting business in Glasgow in 1907, he still retained a love for the cave. He occasionally returned to guide tours during the crowded summer months and on special occasions. Later on, John Nelson sold a collection of both historic and pre-historic items, which he had collected throughout his life, to the National Park Service. Part of this collection included an old iron kettle that was used at the cave entrance as a boiler for gunpowder during the War of 1812. There is a place in the cave named after John known as "Nelson's Domes."

GUIDE, MATT BRANSFORD, 1914. A third generation of the Bransford family appeared at the cave when Louis (1876–1948) and Matt (1882–1960) (above), the sons of Henry, began guiding. Louis guided between 1895 and 1939, and Matt guided between 1905 and 1937. As a boy Matt was a lunch carrier in the cave, making his first trip in 1897. Visitors knew him as conservative, polite, and well educated. Matt's ambition for over three decades was centered on two things: his church and Mammoth Cave. "I have studied the cave. I have lived with it. It has been my life's work and I am proud of it," he said. Matt was awarded a gold medal for his torch throwing in 1913. It was said that he could walk down the steps at the "Ruins of Karnak," throw a flare into a hole in the wall 80 feet away and under a waterfall, and never stop walking. A fourth generation of the Bransford family includes Clifton and Elzie, the sons of Louis, and Arthur, Eddie, and George, the nephews of Louis and Matt.

YOURS TRULY, MATT BRANSFORD, GUIDE, 1905. On the back of this Matt Bransford's guide card was a message from Zemmie Bransford, his wife. The message reads, "Dear Friend, I am send [sic] picture of my husband who showed you through the cave. I arrived home on the 20th of this month and had a fine time. Hoping to see you again. Yours truly, Zemmie Bransford."

MR. M.W. BRANSFORD, C. 1927. Matt Bransford and his wife Zemmie had a large residence, known as Bransford's Resort, which accommodated African-American visitors and the African-American servants of white guests to Mammoth Cave. Guests of their resort received these guide cards as mementos. Matt proudly noted that he was a third-generation cave guide. In all, four generations of the Bransford family guided tours at Mammoth Cave for over 100 years.

GUIDES AND HOTEL AGENTS, 1905. This photograph shows the staff at Mammoth Cave in 1905. From left to right are Ed Bishop, guide; Josh Wilson, guide; Will Bransford, guide; Henry Gossom, hotel clerk; Dr. Willis Ranshaw, hotel operator; Louis Charlet, hotel manager; John Nelson, guide; Matt Bransford, guide; and Bob Lively, guide.

GROUP OF MAMMOTH CAVE GUIDES, 1931. Very few photographs of the cave guides together as a group exist. This photograph, taken in front of the old Guide House, shows several generations of guides from Mammoth Cave. From left to right are the following: (seated) Will Bransford, Bob Lively, Matt Bransford, John Hunter, Schuyler Hunt, and Louis Bransford; (standing) Elzie Bransford, Lester Coats, Leon Hunt, Lyman Cutliff, Lloyd Wilson, George Bransford, Lester Carney, Clifton Bransford, Arthur Bransford, Young Hunt, Charlie Hunt, Leo Hunt, Louis Brown, and Cebert Wilson.

VETERAN GUIDES, 1931. Guides carried hand-held, open-flame lard oil lanterns before the installation of electric lights in the cave, but these only illuminated a limited area. Early cave guides soon perfected the art of torch throwing. Flaming cloth torches were tossed on ledges high above the floor in order to illuminate the far reaches of the cave. Guides competed with each other to hit difficult shots. The practice of flare or torch throwing was part of the Mammoth Cave guides' daily routine up until 1991. It was then discontinued to prevent damage to the cave. This photograph shows five of the older generation of cave guides with lanterns and torch sticks. Each of these veteran guides has between 25 to 40 years of guiding experience at Mammoth Cave. From left to right are John "Mutch" Hunter, Bob Lively, William Bransford, Matt Bransford, and Schuyler Hunt.

ENTERING MAMMOTH CAVE, NOVEMBER 12, 1921. Group photographs were taken in front of the historic entrance to Mammoth Cave beginning in the early 1900s until the 1970s. As they were touring below, the photographs were developed and available for purchase once the tourists returned to the surface. These souvenirs offered a long-lasting remembrance of the cave. Considering the number of tourists who have visited Mammoth Cave during the 70 or so years when these pictures were taken, a large number of these one-of-a-kind pictures can be found today in family collections all over the world. Pictures dated on the back (like the one above) make them even more interesting. Early tour photographs were taken by photographers Stephens and Barry (1900–1904), Harry Pinson (1905–1916), and Joe McDaniels (1919–1949).

Before Entering Mammoth Cave c. 1920. The most memorable man to take group photographs at Mammoth Cave was Joseph McDaniels, the official photographer for 30 years. It has been stated that at least one million visitors have taken home pictures McDaniels took of them at the cave entrance. McDaniels started working as a bellboy at the Mammoth Cave Hotel in 1883. For the next 36 years he worked around the hotel and grounds as a porter, waiter, and assistant cook. He served two years as an apprentice guide but his actual guiding days were few. In 1919, McDaniels and his staff began taking pictures of parties before entering the cave. He used a box camera for all those years and never approved of modern cameras. This is one of many photographs taken by Joe McDaniels.

AT THE ENTRANCE, C. 1920. Early trips into Mammoth Cave were quite an adventure. Before the Civilian Conservation Corps came to improve trails in the 1930s, there was a good chance of getting dirty going through the cave. The hotel provided guests a change of clothes in preparation for the cave tour. The men dressed in jackets, heavy boots, a cloth cap, and woolen pants. The ladies' outfits consisted of a bloomer or Turkish dress. The dress was either plain or fancifully trimmed to suit the wearer. An average trip into Mammoth Cave would last between 4 and 12 hours. Before 1909, there were two tours through the cave, the Short Route (7 miles) and the Long Route (16 miles). After 1909, there were four tours through the cave.

AT THE ENTRANCE TO MAMMOTH CAVE, C. 1920. There were five entrances to Mammoth Cave used for various tours by 1931. They were the Historic Entrance, the New Entrance (opened in 1921), Frozen Niagara Entrance (1924), Violet City Entrance (1931), and the Carmichael Entrance (1931). It has been written that the first crude electric lights were put in Mammoth Cave in 1917. Electric lights were also installed in the first 3,000 feet of the new Carmichael Entrance in 1931. By 1947, the Frozen Niagara section had electric lights and by 1951, the Historic Entrance section had them too. In that same year, a program was started to put lights in all the different trips through the cave except for the Echo River section, where electric wiring would be impractical due to flooding. Notice the types of lanterns used during the 1920s and 1930s and shown in these tour photographs.

At the Entrance of the Mammoth Cave of Kentucky, c. 1930. According to a 1901 guidebook of the cave, regular trips were made daily year-round starting at 9 a.m. and 1 p.m.— regardless of whether there were 1 or 100 visitors at the cave. During the 1920s and 1930s, a trip through the cave could be made as late as 7:30 in the evening.

Mammoth Cave, August 24, 1936. This tour took the new all-day trip that had just started in 1935. They entered through the Historic Entrance and came out the Frozen Niagara Entrance for a seven-mile tour. This tour was offered until 1966, when it was discontinued because of the annual flooding of the underground rivers.

AT THE ENTRANCE, NOVEMBER 27, 1940. Group photographs were taken of visitors standing up or sitting on the ground. The tour seating area was built in front of the cave entrance around 1908. Occasionally guides would pose in the photographs with tourists. Guides Cebert Wilson and Leo Hunt (back row, far right) led this group.

THE MAMMOTH CAVE DONKEY, C. 1908. This photograph, showing a party of guests in cave costume having "The time of our life over again," posed with the donkey in the hotel yard at Mammoth Cave.

WHEN
WILL
WE
THREE
MEET
AGAIN

MRS. & B.J. PALMER, AT
MAMMOUTH-CAVE, KY.
SEPT 15 1910.

MRS. & B.J. PALMER, SEPTEMBER 15, 1910. Many visitors had their photograph taken with the "cave" donkey. Photographer Harry M. Pinson took all the donkey shots from around 1905 until the Mammoth Cave Hotel caught fire in 1916. Pinson accepted a position as photographer at Mammoth Cave under hotel lessee Dr. Willis Renshaw and cave owner Albert Covington Janin. As noted by a visitor to the cave, "A bower of cedars is near the photographer's office and before this the cave donkey stands daily for dozens to have their pictures made while reposing on his comfortable back." This couple wrote, "This is how we looked when away."

MAMMOTH CAVE, JUNE 16, 1916. Outside, in back of the Mammoth Cave Hotel, stood the donkey. Pinson had a painted cave motif background and took photographs of guests on top of the donkey. These guests are still dressed in their cave costumes provided to protect their fine clothing. This photograph was taken just six months before the old hotel burnt to the ground.

PATH LEADING TO THE MOUTH OF CAVE, 1866. The ringing of a bell at the old hotel was the sign that a cave tour was about to begin. The guide stood on the porch and waited for his party of guests to arrive. Behind the Mammoth Cave Hotel and through its garden began a narrow path winding down a dark ravine, which led to Mammoth Cave.

GOING IN, 1908. According to legend, a hunter named Houchins discovered the cave *c.* 1797 when he chased a wounded bear into its natural opening. Recorded history of the cave goes back to 1798 when 200 acres of land, which included the cave, was surveyed for Valentine Simons. Cave guides Ed Bishop and Matt Bransford lead this cave tour into the Historic Entrance in 1908.

MOUTH OF THE CAVE, 1866. This photograph of the undeveloped Historic Entrance is one of the first photographs made of Mammoth Cave by photographer Charles Waldack in 1866. He took 42 different views with the help of magnesium lights. As a result of Waldack's photographic achievement, noted cave writer Horace C. Hovey honored Waldack with the naming of "Waldach Dome" [sic] in Mammoth Cave.

LOOKING DOWN IN, 1889. A path of rough-cut stone steps led the visitor down from the top left of the Historic Entrance to the bottom right before modern improvements were added.

ENTRANCE TO MAMMOTH CAVE, C. 1905. Steps and handrails were added shortly before 1905. The path now started and stayed on the right side of the sinkhole descending into the cave.

MAMMOTH CAVE, GOING IN

GOING IN, C. 1905. Potter College for Young Ladies of Bowling Green had a school trip to Mammoth Cave each year from 1889 to 1909. This photograph shows a group entering the cave in cave costumes. Rates to see the cave were $2 for any one route and $1 for each additional route.

STAIRWAY AT ENTRANCE TO MAMMOUTH CAVE, KY.

STAIRWAY AT ENTRANCE, 1908. Here a group of women descends the entrance stairway into the cave. According to an 1876 guidebook, "every lady carries a lamp, and in no case, except that of illness, should she take a gentleman's arm. It is fatiguing to both parties, and exceedingly awkward in appearance."

THE IRON GATE, 1889. As the visitor walked into the sinkhole entrance of Mammoth Cave, the lanterns were lit and given to each member of the party, the guide reserving two for himself. A walk of about 100 feet brings the group to a manmade rock wall with an iron gate. No one entered the cave unaccompanied by a guide. Only the manager and guides had a key to the cave.

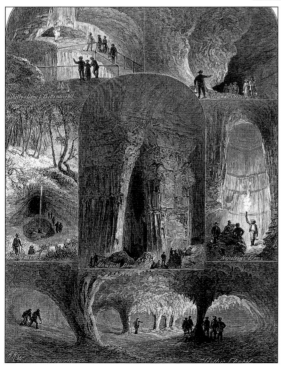

SCENES IN MAMMOTH CAVE, C. 1874. Before the first photograph was taken in Mammoth Cave, woodcuts or engravings were made. Even though they were often exaggerated, they represent the first look into the cave's magnificent depths. The engraving shown at the left was made from a drawing by Alfred R. Waud.

53

SCENES IN MAMMOTH CAVE, C. 1874. Alfred R. Waud was one of the most vivid and productive illustrators of life in the late 19th century. He spent most of his career working for *Harper's Weekly Magazine*, where he established his reputation as a prolific Civil War artist. After the war, Waud made drawings of the South including Mammoth Cave. This engraving was published in *Picturesque America*.

SALT PETRE VATS, 1891. Mammoth Cave played an important role in the War of 1812. These large wooden vats were used during the war for the extraction of nitrates, which were needed to manufacture gunpowder. The "petre dirt" was dumped into vats, where water leached out the salts. Wooden pipes carried the water to the cave for leaching.

ENTRANCE TO GOTHIC AVENUE, 1889. This upper passage of Mammoth Cave is located near the saltpeter pipes. It contains historic signatures as well as formations such as the Bridal Altar, Arm Chair, the Pillar of Hercules, and Lover's Leap. Edwin Booth, the Shakespearean actor (and brother of John Wilkes Booth), performed while perched on the big rock above the stairs in 1876.

KENTUCKY MONUMENT, 1892. Building rock monuments representing a tourist's state in the cave was a common practice. It not only created a lasting memorial to one's home state, but was a common way for cave guides to have tourists clear the rock-strewn trails they walked upon. Of all the many monuments in the cave, it is no surprise that the Kentucky monument is the tallest.

55

THE ALTAR, 1866. The Bridal Altar is a formation made up of three separate stalactites, which form a canopied triangular chamber. These three pillars represent the clergyman and the bride and groom.

THE BRIDAL ALTAR
Copyright, 1908, by H. C. Gan

THE BRIDAL ALTAR, 1908. Approximately 16 weddings were held at the Bridal Altar during the mid-1800s to early 1900s. The first Mammoth Cave wedding was on April 29, 1851. As late as 1924, guidebooks give the number of weddings as 16. This 1908 ceremony features cave guide Matt Bransford to the right.

Marriage Scene, Bridal Altar, Mammoth Cave, Ky.

MARRIAGE SCENE, 1912. Guides often share the story of one special cave wedding. A young girl is said to have made a promise to her dying mother that she would marry no man on the face of the earth. Her marriage ceremony was thus held in Mammoth Cave at the Bridal Altar so that she could marry her beloved—beneath the surface—and still keep the promise she had made to her mother. This 1912 photograph by Alfred V. Oldham shows cave guide Schuyler Hunt at the left.

A WEDDING, NOVEMBER 6, 1915. This picture, by photographer Mary Donna Bullock, shows a wedding party in the cave on November 6, 1915. At one time, Bullock was assistant manager at the Mammoth Cave Hotel. She sold tickets to the cave for 27 years. "Donna's Garden," a passage containing beautiful gypsum formations, was named for Bullock.

THE ARM CHAIR, 1912. Just beyond the Bridal Altar is a formation called the Arm Chair. Early names included the "Devil's Arm Chair" and "Jenny Lind's Arm Chair." Singer Jenny Lind, "The Swedish Nightingale," made this formation world-famous when she sat here during her visit in 1851. Cave guide Schuyler Hunt is shown at the left.

LOVERS' LEAP, 1889. Lovers' Leap is a high, pointed rock at the end of Gothic Avenue. This name was used only figuratively, as there is no documented history of anyone jumping off the rock due to unrequited love.

MARTHA WASHINGTON STATUE, 1889.
William Garvin discovered the "Martha Washington Statue" in 1882. He was alone on Broadway, a main passageway, headed back towards the entrance when he saw a white light that resembled a woman. As he got closer to the apparition, he realized that the light came from around the bend of the next passage and was from lanterns of an approaching tour. The illusion was recreated for tours that followed and named for its resemblance to the original first lady.

THE ACUTE ANGLE, 1889. An approximate 70-degree turn in the main passageway serves to disorient visitors and was a noted point of reference on early tours.

THE HUT, 1889. The hut is a silent reminder of the years 1842 and 1843 when cave owner John Croghan set up a medical experiment hoping that the cave's constant temperature of 54 degrees would have a healing effect on patients suffering from tuberculosis. The experiment went down in medical history as one of the many examples of how *not* to cure tuberculosis. Croghan himself died of the disease in 1849.

STAR CHAMBER, 1892. This is one of the most widely known features of Mammoth Cave. Light reflected from bits of gypsum in the ceiling cast a realistic twinkling effect from above. The source of the light is the cave guide's concealed lantern.

STAR CHAMBER, 1908. Daybreak and sunrise appear in an illusion in the Star Chamber when the guide carries his lantern from one place in the cave toward the seated party. The lantern is at first dimmed, but is gradually brightened as he approaches them. From left to right (standing and seated) in the Star Chamber are guides Bob Lively, Matt Bransford, and Ed Bishop.

THE GIANT'S COFFIN, 1889. This large rock is shaped like a coffin. It is 40 feet long, 20 feet wide, and 16 feet high. Behind this immense piece of limestone is the main path that leads to the river and beyond.

DESERTED CHAMBER, 1866. Photography at Mammoth Cave was extremely difficult and expensive in 1866. By trial and error, photographers attempted to take the best photograph possible under the worst conditions. People had to stand perfectly still while the photograph was taken to avoid blurring the image. The guide in this picture is entering the chamber from the narrow passage beneath the Giant's Coffin. The cloud above him is smoke from the magnesium tapers which were used as a light source.

THE BOTTOMLESS PIT, 1889. Stephen Bishop and a visitor from Georgetown first crossed the Bottomless Pit with two cedar-pole ladders on October 20, 1838. By crossing this pit, which is now known to be 105 feet deep, a major portion of the cave was found for further exploration. Stephen also prepared the first formal detailed map of the cave.

BEYOND THE "BRIDGE OF SIGHS," 1866. This view shows two guides after having crossed the bridge towards Reveler's Hall and facing the Bottomless Pit.

Copyrighted 1892, by Ben

FAT MAN'S MISERY, 1892. Fat Man's Misery is a narrow, winding channel that is over 236 feet long and changes direction many times. Passing through this part of the cave is a challenge for people of all sizes.

HEAD OF ECHO RIVER, 1892. Mammoth Cave guide William Garvin leads a party to Echo River, which is 360 feet underground.

ON ECHO RIVER, 1891. Mammoth Cave guides Henry Bransford (front), William Garvin (at rear), and guests are traveling on Echo River in the cave. To demonstrate the "echo" effect, guides sang a song, and occasionally the tourists would join in as well.

BOAT RIDE ON ECHO RIVER, 1900. Mammoth Cave guides John Nelson (front of boat) and Josh Wilson (rear of boat) are escorting a party of tourists across Echo River. This was necessary to travel from one part of the cave to another. John Nelson once saved a party of guests from drowning in Echo River on January 17, 1904. The river was high that day and every man's head hit the roof of the cave. One man gestured how much higher the cave roof needed to be, and in doing so, pushed the bow of the boat under water. The 17 passengers floundered until John Nelson pulled them to safety on the mud bank.

ON ECHO RIVER, 1908. Guide Matt Bransford is standing in the boat on the left and using a horn to demonstrate the "echo" of Echo River. The river level changed according to the season and recent rainfall, and was sometimes so high that it was impassable by boat. Guests often had to bend low in the boat when water came too close to the ceiling of the cave.

DINNER IN WASHINGTON HALL, 1900. Early trips into Mammoth Cave took anywhere from 4 to 12 hours. On the longer trips, each guide would carry a food basket filled with foods such as fried chicken, apples, biscuits, and wine. Cans of oil were also kept in this section of the cave for refilling the lamps. Guides John Nelson (third from left) and Josh Wilson (second from left) feed a party in the cave in a room known as Washington Hall.

DINING IN GREAT RELIEF, 1866. Various places were chosen in the cave to feed the guests. This area is just beyond Fat Man's Misery, and it was a relief to rest after that part of the journey. Here one of the guides is pouring some of Kentucky's famous bourbon whiskey for the additional relief of his guests.

DINNER IN THE CAVE, 1892. This eating place is beyond Echo River. Shown here are guides William Garvin (standing in back at right) and Josh Wilson (with arm across table).

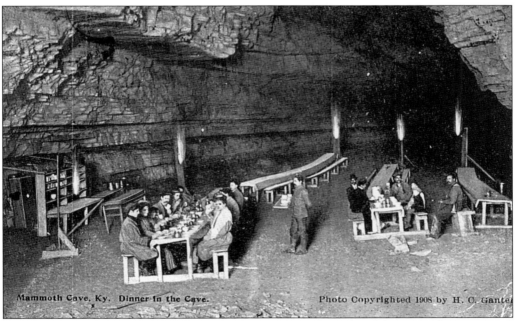

Mammoth Cave, Ky. Dinner In the Cave.　　　　　Photo Copyrighted 1908 by H. C. Ganter

DINNER IN THE CAVE, 1908. Audubon Avenue is just to the right of the Rotunda Room, near the entrance to the cave. Large banquets were set up here. Guests were served on hotel linens by candlelight, and then were taken on a cave tour. Guide Matt Bransford is standing near the center of the room while his tour dines.

A Banquet Scene, 1915. Audubon Avenue could be draped and decorated for special occasions and as many as 200 guests could be served at one time. The food was brought down in the cave from the Mammoth Cave Hotel. Guide Ed Bishop is seated at the front left with this group.

The Snowball Room, 1889. Beautiful gypsum crystals on the ceiling and walls of this room look like snowballs. This room was made into a dining room in 1935. Cave tours stop to eat here today.

044. Lower Passage Opening into Cleveland's Cabinet. Note the Cave is just two stories at this Point, Mammoth Cave, Kentucky

LOWER PASSAGE OPENING INTO CLEVELAND'S CABINET, 1889. Cleveland's Cabinet is one of the most beautiful passages in Mammoth Cave, displaying an abundance of gypsum flowers. It was discovered in July, 1841. Guide Ed Bishop is shown on the right.

THE CORKSCREW, NEAR MIDDLE, 1891. Instead of retracing one's steps back to Fat Man's Misery, the thrilling but occasionally difficult Corkscrew was the main and quickest way back to the entrance of the cave. Guide William Garvin is shown on the bottom ladder.

EXIT OF CORKSCREW INTO MAIN CAVE, 1889. This is the exit of the famous Corkscrew into the main passageway of Mammoth Cave. From here it is a short walk back to the entrance of the cave. Guide William Garvin leads the way out.

COMING OUT, 1908. The cave tour is coming out of the natural cave entrance after a long but pleasant journey through the cave. According to an old guidebook, "It is not an uncommon occurrence for a person in delicate health to accomplish a journey of twenty miles in the cave, without suffering from fatigue, who could not be prevailed upon to walk a distance of three miles on the surface of the earth." They still have one long steep hill to climb back to the hotel.

WORLD'S FAIR, 1893.
The state of Kentucky had a pavilion in the Mines and Mining Building at the 1893 Chicago World's Fair. The building featured a replica section of Mammoth Cave. The *Manufacturer and Builder* magazine gave the following review of the exhibit: "There has been arranged a room in exact representation of one of the most famous chambers of the Mammoth Cave. This room is lined with stalactites and crystals, and upon its walls are hung pictures of the striking features to be found within the celebrated cave. A veteran cave guide is in constant attendance." Many of the beautiful gypsum flowers were shown at the exhibit. The management of the cave, under the direction of Henry C. Ganter, stripped an area off Cleaveland Avenue known as "Charlotte's Grotto." The gypsum flower specimens and the Mammoth (Salt's) Cave mummy "Little Al" were brought to the fair by cave guide William Bransford to help promote business. The top part of the photograph shows the "Coal Arch Entrance to Kentucky" exhibit. Guide Ed Bishop is in the bottom part of the photograph at the entrance to Mammoth Cave.

WORLD'S FAIR, CHICAGO, 1893.

KENTUCKY

COAL ARCH—entrance to KY. Exhibit

MOUTH OF MAMMOTH CAVE—Kentucky

KENTUCKY COLUMBIAN EXHIBIT
Department of Mines and Forestry, Chicago, Ill.

CORBITT-SKIDMORE CO.   PRINTERS AND ENGRAVERS, CHICAGO.

ROTC Camp, c. 1930. During the 1930s, the Reserve Officers Training Corps (ROTC) visited and set up camp at Mammoth Cave. The top photograph shows tents laid out upon the hotel grounds. The bottom photograph shows a group on the path just before reaching the Historic Entrance to Mammoth Cave. The official ROTC photographer, Kirkpatrick, took the photograph.

Two

New Entrance to Mammoth Cave

New Entrance Hotel Party, c. 1924. The Delco Light Convention posed for a photograph in front of the New Entrance Hotel. Delco associates put electric lights in the cave and there was a sign placed above the New Entrance stating, "Delco Light Used Here." "Brilliantly Illumed by Electric Lights" was used in brochures advertising the cave.

Frozen Niagara

New Entrance

TO

Mammoth Cave

75 feet in heighth　　　**50 feet in width**

NIAGARA FALLS, REPRODUCED IN ONYX

To Cave Visitors and Tourists:

"We do not show any of that part of the Cave, which prior to 1907 was generally known to the public as "Mammoth Cave." That portion of the Cave can be seen only through the old entrance."

NEW ENTRANCE TO MAMMOTH CAVE, C. 1924. George Morrison came to the Mammoth Cave area in 1915. After hearing stories that Mammoth Cave extended beyond the property line of the Mammoth Cave Estate, he hired crews to run illegal surveys. In 1921, Morrison, an oil driller by trade, blasted his way into the cave on land he controlled. He then improved the underground trails and built a hotel nearby. Morrison called his cave the "New Entrance to Mammoth Cave" because he claimed he was showing part of Mammoth Cave. The New Entrance location was on the same road as Mammoth Cave, only closer, so Morrison created competition when he started setting up roadside signs. This took a lot of business away from Mammoth Cave, and since the management was not happy about this, they went to federal court over the matter. It was decided by the courts that Morrison was indeed showing a part of Mammoth Cave, and thus he could use the name Mammoth Cave. However, Morrison had to put in his advertisements that he was only showing the part of Mammoth Cave found after 1907.

NEW ENTRANCE HOTEL, C. 1924. The New Entrance Hotel was built in 1923 and was under the management of William O'Neal. The hotel advertised, "good rooms, good beds, and good meals" at the rate of $3.50 to $4 per day on the American plan, and was located at the only cave entrance that could be reached on a hard road at the time. This was a considerable advantage over the other caves that could be reached only by dirt roads. The hotel was demolished in 1945.

FROZEN NIAGARA ENTRANCE, C. 1930. The Frozen Niagara Entrance to Mammoth Cave opened in 1924 and was used as an exit after entering the cave from the New Entrance. In 1931, both the New and Frozen Niagara Entrances became part of the new Mammoth Cave National Park. Here the ROTC members are in front of the Frozen Niagara Entrance.

GIANT STAIRWAY, 1922. George Morrison leads a group down the long wooden stairway he constructed into the sinkhole entrance to New Entrance Cave. According to the photograph, the giant stairway leads "from the Camel's Spring, across the 110 foot pit to the N.Y. Subway, at bottom of Corkscrew."

DINNER PARTY, 1922. Like Mammoth Cave, the New Entrance section of the cave was also extensive, and food was served during tours. George Morrison (second from the right) joined this party for dinner 360 feet below the surface after being in the cave for three hours.

BOAT RIDE ON CRYSTAL RIVER, 1924.
The Mammoth Cave Development
Company (New Entrance) capitalized
on many crowd-pleasing features
already found in Mammoth Cave. This
boat ride was actually on a very small
manmade lake, but was advertised
as "The Most Beautiful River Ever
Discovered." The photograph also
shows the illusion/formation known as
"September Morn, the Bathing Beauty,
the Masterpiece of all Cave Statues."

FROZEN NIAGARA, C. 1930. The
name Frozen Niagara was given to this
formation due to its resemblance to the
mighty Niagara Falls. This photograph
was taken before steps or handrails were
installed down to the bottom of the
formation. The ROTC group seated at
the top provides a scale to show how
large this formation really is.

FROZEN NIAGARA, C. 1935. The Frozen Niagara is approximately 40 feet wide and 75 feet high. The huge formation was the main attraction and climax of a trip through the New Entrance to Mammoth Cave. This photograph shows part of the handrails that were put in by the Civilian Conservation Corps (CCC) during the mid-1930s.

SEE THE LITTLE GIRL TURNED TO STONE, 1922. After visitors had finished their tour of the New Entrance, they were returned to the cave office and shown the mummified remains of a little girl. She was named the "Little Lady of the Cave" and was one of George Morrison's attractions.

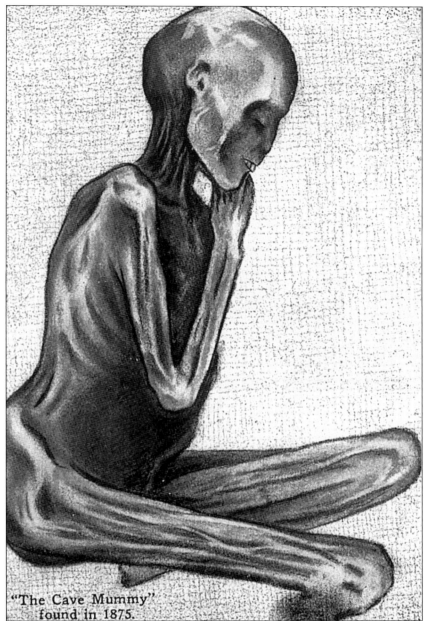

"The Cave Mummy" found in 1875.

THE CAVE MUMMY C. 1910. The mummy was originally found in Salts Cave in 1875 by Mammoth Cave guides Tom Lee, John Lee, and William Cutliff. After the mummy was discovered, she was exhibited at the Smithsonian Institution, Procter's Cave, Grand Avenue Cave, Mammoth Cave, and the New Entrance to Mammoth Cave. Morrison obtained the mummy from former Mammoth Cave manager Henry Ganter after he died. For a time, the mummy was called "Little Alice," but after an examination in 1958 it was actually found to be a boy. In 1935, the mummy "Lost John" was discovered in Mammoth Cave by guides Lyman Cutliff and Grover Campbell. It was found under a six-ton block of limestone, two-and-a-half miles into the cave.

C.C.C. CO. 543, CAMP NEW ENTRANCE, MAMMOTH CAVE, KY.

CCC Co. 543, Camp New Entrance, c. 1935. The Civilian Conservation Corps (CCC) was sent to Mammoth Cave in 1933 to prepare the area to become a national park. Four camps were set up, which housed 200 to 250 enrollees. Company 510 (Camp 1) was located near Crystal Cave. Company 543 (Camp 2) is shown here and was located near the New Entrance to Mammoth Cave. Company 582 (Camp 3) was located on Joppa Ridge. Company 516 (Camp 4) was located on the north side of the Green River. Some of the improvements to the park made by the CCC included landscaping; surveying; tree planting; a sewage, telephone, and water system; roads; surface and cave trails; and general cleanup. All four camps divided the workload at Mammoth Cave, although a few of the camps did specialize in certain areas.

Three

GREAT ONYX CAVE
AND COLOSSAL CAVE

GREAT ONYX CAVE HOTEL, 1920. As with other caves in the Mammoth Cave area, Great Onyx Cave had its own modern hotel to accommodate visitors. The hotel slogan was, "A trip any time, a meal any time, a bed any time, we never sleep."

Entrance to the Great Onyx Cave, KY.
Copyrighted 1917 by L.P.Edwards.
One of the Greatest Caverns Known,
Greatest Variety of Fantastical Formation

ENTRANCE TO THE GREAT ONYX CAVE, 1917. The Great Onyx Cave was privately owned and discovered on June 12, 1915. A clogged spring was blasted open while seeking water for a plow horse and the cave was revealed. The cave and hotel were owned and operated by L.P. Edwards. After Edwards died, the cave was passed on to his daughter Lucy Cox, her husband W. Perry Cox, and her nephew Harry Bush. There has been debate over who actually found Great Onyx Cave. Some say Edwards did and others say it was Edmund Turner. The story goes that Turner made a deal with Edwards: if Edwards would give him one-half interest in the cave, he would show him where to dig. They both came to a verbal agreement and Great Onyx Cave was found and opened. The cave was sold to the National Park Service in 1961 and is now part of Mammoth Cave National Park.

GREAT ONYX FORMATIONS, 1915 AND 1916. As part of the 50-50 agreement between Edwards and Turner, postcards were published in 1915 that featured both Turner's and Edwards' names, as on the one to the right showing Explorer's Pass. Soon after the discovery, Turner died, and Edwards immediately claimed that he discovered Great Onyx Cave. Published postcards of the cave between 1916 and 1920 did not include Turner's name. It seems that Edwards was trying to hide the fact that Turner ever had any part in the discovery of Great Onyx Cave. The photograph below of the Alabaster Stalactite shows only Edwards' name in 1916.

Explorer's Pass , Great Onyx Cave, Ky.
Copyrighted 1915 by L.P.Edwards & Edmund Turner.

Alabaster Stalactite, Great Onyx Cave, Ky.
Copyrighted 1916 by L.P.Edwards.

RUSTIC PATH, 1919. An early brochure of the cave reads, "Below the modern hotel and free tourist camp . . . forest trails lead through woodlands, studded with wildflowers, and water sports on Green River." In this picture, a tour group descends the steep rustic path leading to the entrance of Great Onyx Cave.

Rustic Path to Great Onyx Cave, Ky.

19 Ⓒ 19

L.P.Edwards
11010

A GROUP OF GUIDES, C. 1922. Tours were given at Great Onyx Cave any hour of the day or night, from 30 minutes to 3 1/2 hours in duration. The guides above are unidentified, but a list of prominent guides at Great Onyx Cave from 1924 included Willard Holden, Roe Estes, Lee Wood, Hebert Gore, Sylvester Lee, Charley Dennison, Bud Davis, and James Crinshaw.

GREAT ONYX CAVE, C. 1930. Tour pictures were occasionally taken inside the cave. Outside pictures were popular at Mammoth Cave, but underground photographs were a different marketing approach at Great Onyx Cave. The cave formations in the background may have attracted tourists to buy the unique photographs.

VIEW IN THE COLONNADE, 1920. Great Onyx Cave was considered a beautiful cave with dense formations, but it was past the main entrance road to Mammoth Cave. Extensive advertising helped the cave to draw in tourists. There were a lot of small caves on the highway with names similar to Great Onyx Cave, but tourists were advised to follow directions and keep on driving "to get to the one and only Great Onyx Cave."

LUCIKOVAH RIVER, C. 1924. A manmade river was built in 1924 and new flyers were immediately published to announce the new "discovery," now with boat rides any hour day or night. The top photograph shows a portion of the new "Lucikovah River" and the bottom advertisement announces the new discovery. Great Onyx Cave was known as the formation cave of the National Park Area and was valued at $398,000 in 1924.

GREAT ONYX CAVE
Announces New Discovery
Added to original routes making more cave trip at no additional cost. - NEW UNDERGROUND RIVER TRIP is easy to reach - BOAT RIDES ANY HOUR day or night.
Trips Arranged from 30 minutes to 2 1-2 hours

CAUTION!
If you desire to see the World Famous Great Onyx Cave DRIVE TO CAVE CITY and follow Highway No. 70 to Mammoth Cave. Turn to right at archway and follow signs to GREAT ONYX CAVE.

-- READ OTHER SIDE --

EDWARD'S VALLEY, 1916. Great Onyx Cave also had big rooms similar to those in Mammoth and the New Entrance Caves. Edward's Valley marks the furthest point reached in the first exploration after its 1915 discovery. The cave remains one of the few in the area that is still not physically connected with Mammoth Cave.

COLOSSAL CAVE, 1908. Lute and Henry Lee discovered Colossal Cave in 1895 by working their way down a sinkhole. Both brothers made explorations of the cave and later sold their interest to L.W. Hazen. Hazen was employed by the L&N Railroad and became manager of Colossal Cave. Here visitors are shown ready to tour Colossal Cave.

COLOSSAL CAVE ENTRANCE, C. 1900. The first advertising of Colossal Cave as a show cave was in 1897 under the name Colossal Cavern Company. The cave enjoyed some success but by 1910 only a few were visiting the cave. By the 1920s, it was closed. This photograph shows the sinkhole entrance to Colossal Cave. A roof over the entrance protected visitors from the elements of weather.

COLOSSAL CAVE TEAMS, 1908. James M. Hunt became manager of Colossal Cave after Hazen was discharged. Hunt was stationed at the Mammoth Cave Hotel in order to arrange transportation for the visitors to the cave. Wagons waited to take tourists from Mammoth Cave to Colossal Cave.

Cave Explorers making trip across the mountains from Mammoth to Colossal Cave, Kentucky.

MAKING THE TRIP TO COLOSSAL CAVE, 1908. The entrance to Colossal Cave was about one-and-a-half miles from the Mammoth Cave Hotel, at the foot of a steep hill facing west. The road to the cave was not well traveled in 1908. Cave explorers made the rugged trip "across the mountains from Mammoth to Colossal Cave."

READY FOR A TRIP THROUGH THE CAVERN C. 1914. Guided trips through Colossal Cave cost $2, which included transportation from the Mammoth Cave Hotel to the cavern and back. The cave trip lasted about four hours and could be made at any hour of the day. The photograph shows a group getting ready to tour Colossal Cave. The guide is on the far right, dressed in a white jacket.

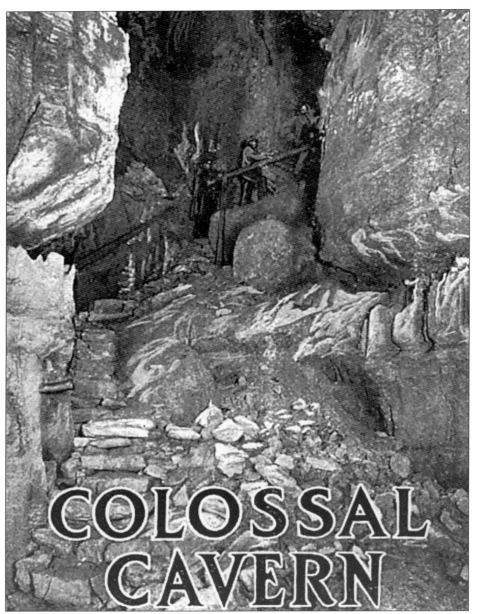

COLOSSAL CAVERN

COLOSSAL CAVERN BROCHURE, C. 1915. The following description was taken from the only promotional brochure made of the cave: "The remarkable cavern was found but a few years ago and stands practically the same now as when first discovered. It contains some of the finest underground passages found in any cavern. As yet this remarkable wonder has not been fully explored but there are some seven miles now open to the public. Do not fail to visit it, the trip from Cascade Hall to the bottom of Colossal Dome is probably the most wonderful that can be made by human being." At the time it was customary for all visitors to write their names in what is known as "Registration Hall." According to an account of the cave, "From the number of times that some person's had registered, I concluded that a primary election had been held in there at some time."

Four

FLOYD COLLINS' CRYSTAL CAVE AND SAND CAVE

OUTSIDE LOOKING IN, C. 1925. Floyd Collins discovered Crystal Cave in 1917 on his father's farm while looking for an animal trap in a sinkhole. Removing rocks as he dug his way in, he felt cool air coming out. As Floyd continued to crawl, he discovered big passageways and beautiful white gypsum. Floyd called his new discovery the Great Crystal Cave. This photograph shows the Great Crystal Cave sinkhole entrance.

FLOYD COLLINS, AGE 37, 1924. Floyd Collins was one of the most prominent cave explorers of the Mammoth Cave region. He made the statement that all the caves in the area were connected long before this was discovered to be true. His explorations laid the foundation for others to discover that Mammoth Cave was the longest cave in the world. Crystal Cave, Colossal Cave, Salts Cave, and others were proven to be connected to Mammoth Cave by 1972. At a very young age, Floyd wandered around the sinkholes of his father's farm, looking for a cave to rival Mammoth. His interest in caves was an obsession and he spent much of his free time caving alone or with his brothers. Floyd Collins had no fear of exploring the most difficult cave passages, and few people could match his persistence and endurance. Floyd had this photograph taken as a Crystal Cave tour guide.

Entrance,
Great Crystal Cave, Ky.

GREAT CRYSTAL CAVE, C. 1920. Soon after the discovery of Crystal Cave, Floyd and his family made improvements in preparation of opening the cave to the public. A stairway had to be built down into the sinkhole entrance. Leveled underground trails also had to be built. Shown here are two rare photographs of the entrance to Great Crystal Cave. The top photograph is of the entrance looking in; the bottom photograph is looking out of the entrance opening.

Entrance, Looking Out,
Great Crystal Cave, Ky.

NANNIE RAMSEY'S FLOWER GARDEN, C. 1920. Mr. Lee Collins, Floyd's father, is in a section of the cave that displays the beautiful white gypsum flowers.

CRYSTAL SPRINGS, C. 1922. When business was slow at Great Crystal Cave, Floyd would take the time to explore with his brothers, Homer and Marshall. But most of the time, he was alone in his travels. Floyd Collins is shown at the top left holding a coal oil lantern and taking a water break in Crystal Cave.

EXAMINING BONES, 1922. Even though Floyd's cave was a work of art, it was not a moneymaker. The cave had no hotels like the other caves. Crystal Cave was also the last cave on the main road. Tourists had to pass New Entrance, Mammoth, and Great Onyx before they came to Crystal Cave. Floyd continued his explorations in an attempt to find a more profitable cave to show to tourists. He is seen here examining bones discovered in an adjacent cave nearby. He eventually found a small cave closer to the main road on the land of friend Bee Doyle. While exploring the newly found cavern, his foot was trapped by a rock dislodged from the ceiling.

RESCUING FLOYD COLLINS, 1925. The news of Floyd's entrapment quickly captivated the public attention in newspapers across the country. The press named the crevice Sand Cave and for two weeks reporters from everywhere showed up at the scene. Attempts to free Floyd were made by his brothers and William "Skeets" Miller, a reporter from Louisville. Because of the limited space in the tight passageway between Floyd and his rescuers, no one could get him out. The photograph shows a large tarpaulin covering the entrance to Sand Cave to protect the workers from the weather.

SAND CAVE AREA, 1925. After the press arrived, people flocked to the area. Automobiles were parked anywhere space was available. The scene around the cave turned into a carnival-like atmosphere. The top photograph shows a number of cars parked in an open field. The bottom photograph shows a group of people around the rescue area. Notice the Red Cross tent that was set up.

GUARDS TENT, SAND CAVE, 1925. Within a week, the National Guard had to be brought in to control the large crowds of people and cars around the cave during the rescue effort. They set up a number of tents across the rescue area.

BEE DOYLE, 1925. This photograph, taken after Floyd's entrapment, shows Bee Doyle in the rocky slot of the Sand Cave shaft to demonstrate Floyd Collins's position as he was trapped. The awkward position of Floyd in the cave made it difficult for anyone to reach him with food and drink. Rescue attempts were physically demanding and mentally exhausting.

SHAFT AT SAND CAVE, 1925. After rock falls blocked the passageway to Floyd, a vertical shaft was built down to him. On February 16, Floyd Collins was reached, but it was too late. This photograph shows Bee Doyle at the top of the shaft after the removal of Floyd Collins's body from Sand Cave.

MR. BRENNEN who worked 16 days and nights to rescue Floyd Collins from the cave at Sand Cave, Ky., he being the only man to lay hands on Mr. Collins, after his death.

GIVE WHAT YOU CAN.

ED BRENNER, 1925. Miner Ed Brenner was the first man down in the shaft to reach Floyd Collins. This picture card of Ed was a handout. It seems Mr. Brenner wanted financial compensation for his rescue efforts and had this card printed. It reads, "Mr. Brennen [sic] who worked 16 days and nights to rescue Floyd Collins from the cave at Sand Cave, Ky., he being the only man to lay hands on Mr. Collins, after his death. Give What You Can."

RAISING THE BODY, APRIL 23, 1925. This photograph shows the removal of Floyd Collins's body from Sand Cave on April 23, 1925. Even though Floyd was found dead on February 16, he was not brought to the surface until April 23 because of the cave's instability.

PAYING LAST RESPECTS, APRIL 23, 1925. Rev. R.B. Neal offers a prayer after Floyd's body was removed from Sand Cave. It was said 5,000 people viewed his body the morning he was brought out of the cave. During the past 75 years since his death, the body of Floyd Collins has been buried five times.

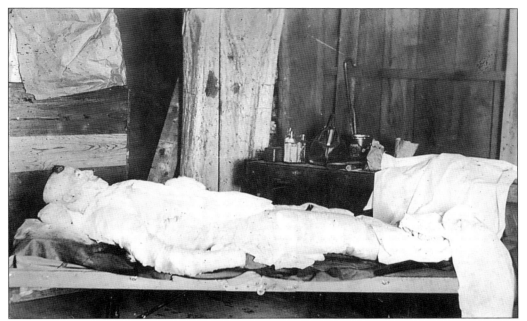

AT THE UNDERTAKERS, APRIL 24, 1925. Floyd Collins's body is laid out at the undertaker's parlor in Cave City, Kentucky after being embalmed. J.T. Geralds was the undertaker. Each of the five times Floyd was buried, the body had to be embalmed and restored.

BEE DOYLE AT SAND CAVE, 1925. Bee Doyle is seen holding the 27-pound rock that pinned Floyd. Bee Doyle briefly operated the Sand Cave area as a tourist attraction to show where Floyd was trapped. The ticket office at the right still exists just outside the boundaries of Mammoth Cave National Park.

WHERE FLOYD COLLINS MET DEATH, 1925. The top photograph shows a group of men at the entrance to Sand Cave after the removal of Floyd Collins. The hoist and bucket was used to bring Floyd up the 70-foot shaft to the surface. The bottom photograph shows the same group of men looking towards the entrance to Sand Cave. Photographer Wade H. Highbaugh of Cave City, Kentucky, was the only photographer to capture the removal of Floyd Collins from Sand Cave. This chapter includes 13 rare photographs of Great Crystal Cave (3) and Sand Cave (10) taken by Highbaugh.

Scenes at Sand Cave, Ky.
where Floyd Collins age 37, was trapped.

Scenes at Sand Cave, K
where Floyd Collins age 37, was trapped

SCENES AT SAND CAVE, 1925. Wade Highbaugh thoroughly documented the area around Sand Cave with pictures after Floyd was brought out. The photograph negatives, thought to have been destroyed, are preserved today by Highbaugh's son Udolf. Visitors today can see the actual place where Floyd Collins was trapped. A short boardwalk path leads to an overlook at the Mammoth Cave park boundary entrance. It is a very gloomy place to visit any time of the day. The top photograph shows the entrance to Sand Cave and the bottom photograph shows the entrance just to the left.

Scenes at Sand Cave, Ky.
where Floyd Collins age 37, was trapped.
(PHOTO BY WADE H.HIGHBAUGH.)

FLOYD COLLINS' CRYSTAL CAVE KENTUCKY

FLOYD COLLINS

200 feet high, 700 feet long, and 100 feet wide—Grand Canyon Avenue, the largest individual underground chamber in the National Park area, with its millions of golden-brown crystal incrustations, is a worthy memorial to its internationally famous discoverer, Floyd Collins. This is the best-lighted and dryest cave in Kentucky.

FLOYD COLLINS' CRYSTAL CAVE, C. 1930. In 1927, Lee Collins (Floyd's father) sold Crystal Cave to Dr. Harry Thomas, a dentist in Horse Cave, Kentucky. Thomas owned two other show caves, Mammoth Onyx and Hidden River Cave. Part of the deal involved having Floyd's remains displayed in a glass coffin and shown to the general public. For the first time, Floyd Collins' Crystal Cave was finally making money. The opportunity to see Floyd as part of the cave attraction was hard to pass up. The description from the brochure states, "In Crystal Cave (the largest formation cave in Kentucky) one may see, combined in one great attraction, Grand Canyon Avenue, Floyd Collins' Memorial, the most graceful of large underground chambers, the largest and most varied deposit of cave gypsum and crystal, and the rarest discovery of fantastic onyx helectite formation on the North American Continent. These features, shown by powerful electric effect, present a never-fading picture of unique delight."

FLOYD COLLINS' TOMB, C. 1940. Floyd Collins' tomb was placed in Grand Canyon in Crystal Cave. Here the casket and tombstone can be seen on the floor of the large canyon passageway. Floyd's body remained in this location until the National Park Service reburied him in 1989 at the Mammoth Cave Baptist Church Cemetery on Flint Ridge Road at Mammoth Cave National Park.

Grand Canyon and Floyd Collins Tomb - Floyd Collins Crystal Cave-Horse Cave, Ky.

Floyd Collins Birthplace - Floyd Collins Crystal Cave - Horse Cave, Ky.

FLOYD COLLINS' BIRTHPLACE, C. 1940. Floyd Collins grew up in this house, which was on land just above the sinkhole entrance to Crystal Cave. Crystal Cave was sold to the National Park Service in 1961 and is now part of Mammoth Cave National Park.

FLOYD COLLINS MONUMENT, C. 1940. A memorial was built to honor Floyd Collins in the city of Horse Cave. The 30-foot tall circular monument was made of stone, and an American flag flew from the top. The base of the monument featured a picture of Floyd on one side and an inscription on the other. The monument was later hit by a truck and destroyed, and all that exists of the monument today is the walkway to the base. The inscription from the monument read, "He lived for an ideal, in search of earthly beauty, this he found in his discovery of Crystal Cave. He died for an ideal, the ideal of service before self." The inscription from his tombstone reads, "Trapped in Sand Cave Jan. 30, 1925, Discovered Crystal Cave, Jan. 18, 1917 Greatest Cave Explorer Ever Known."

Five

HIDDEN RIVER CAVE
MAMMOTH ONYX CAVE
DIAMOND CAVERNS

HIDDEN RIVER CAVE, C. 1920. Hidden River Cave is in the center of downtown Horse Cave, Kentucky. The cave was formerly called Horse Cave, from which the town took its name. Different people have owned the cave from as early as 1795. In 1908, Dr. Harry Thomas bought out the other heirs of his father, G.A. Thomas, and by 1916, the cave was opened to tourists.

ENTRANCE TO HIDDEN RIVER CAVE, C. 1920. The Entrance to Hidden River Cave is just beside the main road in Horse Cave. Dr. Harry Thomas built a long stairway and handrails into the sinkhole entrance, and footbridges were built to cross the river that ran through it. A tennis court was built in the yard in front of the entrance to the cave.

200 FEET BELOW, C. 1920. In 1890, a dam was built in Hidden River Cave and a hydraulic ram was installed. Pumps were added to supply water to the town of Horse Cave in 1892. An electric generator was installed in the cave in 1895. As a result, Horse Cave was the second town in Kentucky to have electricity. The opera house, and Thomas's house, dental office, and store were the first buildings in town to have electricity. Electric lights were also installed in the cave, making it one of the first to have electricity.

ENTRANCE TO HIDDEN RIVER CAVE, C. 1920. The huge cave entrance was boarded up except for a door and windows. Later, an iron gate replaced the wood but still secured the cave. In the 1940s, pollution closed the cave to tours, but today, after a new sewage treatment system was built, the cave is again open to tourists. It is now part of the American Cave Museum.

Central Cave Office and Cavern Gift Shop, on U. S. 31W, Horse Cave, Ky.

CENTRAL CAVE OFFICE, C. 1940. This stone structure served as ticket office and gift shop for Hidden River Cave, Mammoth Onyx Cave, and Floyd Collins' Crystal Cave. The office was just across the road from the Floyd Collins Memorial and Hidden River Cave.

DANCING PAVILION AND ENTRANCE TO MAMMOTH ONYX CAVE, C. 1925. Dr. Harry Thomas opened his second cave, Mammoth Onyx Cave, in 1921. As the story goes, a native maiden named Martha Woodson discovered it in 1799 while picking berries from a hillside. She felt a cool draft of air from the rocks, and with her brothers' help, she was lowered into the sinkhole entrance. According to an early brochure, the cave was called the "only Onyx Cave in Kentucky" and "The Cleanest and Prettiest Cave in the World." It was one of the few in the area that featured electric lights at the time. Assistant geologist Charles H. Richardson claimed in 1922 that "the stalactites and stalagmites are indeed beautiful, and every tourist will be well repaid for his trip through the cave." The stone structure to the left is the back of the entrance to Mammoth Onyx Cave. Today, it is known as Kentucky Caverns.

MOONSHINE STILL AND FOUNTAIN OF YOUTH, C. 1930. Cave owners advertised and displayed many things in their caves in order to draw tourists. Besides the cave formations, a moonshine still (right) and a "Fountain of Youth" (below) were two popular attractions. Wishing wells were a popular way of making additional money for the cave, as tourists were encouraged to throw coins into shallow ponds.

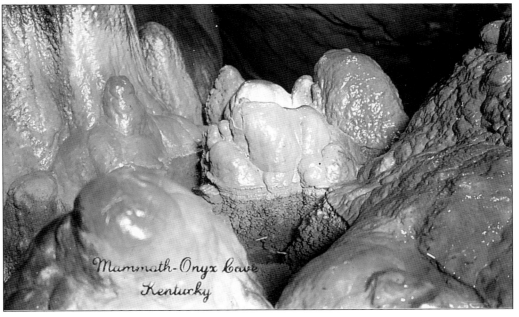

Glasgow Jct., Ky., Routes U.S. 68, U.S. 31 W.

DIAMOND CAVERNS, C. 1930. Diamond Caverns was discovered by a slave on July 14, 1859 and opened to tours in August of that year. It was originally called Richardson Cave, after one of the cave's original explorers. George Procter (the brother of Larkin Procter, who managed Mammoth Cave) was the proprietor of Diamond Caverns. The cave was called "Diamond" because the formations sparkled. Electric lights were installed in 1917, and concrete steps and a bridge were added in 1924. In 1936, the New Discovery passage doubled the length of the cave. The stone arch entrance can be seen just under the building overhang in the center of the photograph.

Birds Eye View Dimond Caverns, Glasgow Jct., Ky., Routes U.S. 68, U.S. 31 W.

BIRDS EYE VIEW, C. 1930. Diamond Caverns was one of the first stops on the Mammoth Cave Railroad in 1886. The cave was located one-and-a-half miles north of the Glasgow Junction Depot. The Procter family owned three caves during the early years of the Mammoth Cave Railroad, including Procter (opened in 1863), Diamond, and Grand Avenue Caves. Prior to 1892, the Mammoth Cave Railroad Company thought Grand Avenue Cave rivaled Mammoth Cave as an underground attraction and built a secondary line of about one mile from Diamond Cave to Grand Avenue Cave. Unfortunately, this line was rarely used. Grand Avenue Cave acquired its commercial fame as a show cave in 1875. The Mammoth Cave Railroad is located just behind the arch in the photograph, in back of the office and entrance building to Diamond Caverns.

ONYX MOUNTAIN BRIDGE, c. 1930. On August 19, 1859, the Kennedy party was the first to take a tour of the caverns under the guidance of Prof. Charles W. Wright. To commemorate the occasion, an inscription was made in marble and placed at the entrance to the cave. One of the footbridges in the decorated cave is shown here.

ONYX HAYSTACK, c. 1930. Early descriptions of the cave claim Diamond Caverns "is Kentucky's Most Beautiful Cave, A Natural Museum in Mountains of Onyx, and An Enchanting Garden of Magnificent Beauty." N.S. Shaler, a Harvard geologist, claims that "Diamond Cave is the most beautiful of the 100 or more I have visited in all parts of the world."

Six

LOST RIVER CAVE

LOST RIVER CAVE ENTRANCE, C. 1908. The Lost River Cave and Valley in Bowling Green has been known for hundreds of years. The first major use of the river was to power a milling machine to making corn meal in the early 1800s. Later, the river was used to power a sawmill.

LOST RIVER INN AND TOURIST CAMP, C. 1930. The old mill was gone by the time of the Civil War and a new one was built in 1874. The mill was constructed above the cave entrance. Flour was ground at the mill and later a distillery produced peach and apple brandy. It was said to be the largest brandy producer in the country. The mill caught fire in 1915 and burnt to the ground. Lost River Cave started operating as a tourist attraction in the 1920s. Tourist cabins and food were available on the road just above the cave entrance. A two-story restaurant, gift shop, and dance club opened in 1926 on the site of the old mill. Many advertising signs were erected in hopes that tourists would stop and see the cave.

LOST RIVER CAVE, C. 1940. A planned amusement park with concessions and rides was to be built next to the restaurant and dance club, but never materialized. In 1935, a filling station was added, as were 12 tourist cabins. Many of the cabins were one-room structures. These two photographs show the main entrance and cave office for Lost River by U.S. Highway 31W. The stone arch entrance to Lost River Cave can be seen in both photographs. At one time, the old mill was located where the cave office building is seen in the bottom photograph.

CAVE OFFICE, C. 1940. The owners of Lost River Cave had this building constructed above the cave for the office and gift shop. They promoted the cave as being the "Hide Out of Jesse James" and "World's Shortest and Deepest River." They even advertised the mummified body of a Native American supposedly found in the cave with the slogan, "See Man that Turned to Stone." This building burned in 1990.

WINDING STAIRWAY, C. 1940. Cave owner W.L. Perkins built a small power plant and powerhouse just in front of the entrance to the cave. A generator was installed in the powerhouse to generate electricity for the nightclub, and a long stairway was built from the stone arch down to the entrance of the cave.

THE OPENING TO LOST RIVER CAVE, C. 1940. Lost River Cave became an underground nightclub in 1934. The cave was open for dancing, dining, and boat rides on the river. Perkins rented the underground nightclub to Jimmy Stewart and Harold Oliphant from 1934 through 1949, and Perkins offered guided tours of the cave during the day. According to a brochure put out by the cave, "They now have an underground night club seventy feet below the level of the ground, over five thousand feet of foot space, which is now used for a dance floor. This being a temperature of sixty degrees makes it a very pleasant, as well as interesting place and is visited by several thousand people annually." The entrance opening shown in both photographs is believed to be one of the largest in the eastern United States.

DANCE PAVILION IN LOST RIVER CAVE, C. 1940. The cool cave was popular with citizens of Warren County as well as tourists traveling through the state, especially during the hot summer months. Food and beverages were served in the cave, and dances held there were often formal events. This view shows the large dance floor, a stone bar in the background, and a stone bandstand where music was played.

WATERFALL IN LOST RIVER CAVE, C. 1940. The underground nightclub closed down in 1949, but tours were still given through the cave until 1960. The Lost River Cave and Valley closed for 30 years, but is open today thanks to an organization called "Friends of Lost River," who restored the cave and valley.

Seven

OTHER CAVES

FIRST ENTRANCE, INDIAN CAVE, C. 1930. Indian Cave was first discovered and exhibited in 1861 as a point of interest when traveling the road from Cave City to Mammoth Cave. It was conveniently located directly on the road for the visitor who only had a few minutes to spare. The proprietor of the cave at that time was Sam B. Young. This postcard was made for the cave in the 1940s and mentions the recent lighting throughout the cave.

ENTRANCE TO WHITE'S CAVE, 1900.
White Cave was another cave owned
by the Mammoth Cave Estate. It is
located about a half-mile from the
entrance to Mammoth Cave. It is
only 200 feet long, but contains some
beautiful white formations. The owners
of Mammoth Cave showed the cave at
different intervals. Visitors to this cave
had to get on their hands and knees
to crawl into the small entrance.

**PILLARS OF SCIENCE, WHITE'S CAVE,
1898.** The white formations found in
White Cave are different from anything
in Mammoth Cave, excepting the Frozen
Niagara area. Since 1850, the cave has
attracted the attention of scientists as well
as tourists. Motion pictures were taken in
the cave in 1915.

TITANIA'S BOWER, GANTER'S CAVE, 1900. Ganter's Cave is three miles south of Mammoth Cave on the north side of the Green River. Access to the cave was made by boat from the Mammoth Cave side of the river. The cave was named for Henry C. Ganter, who managed the Mammoth Cave Estate for many years.

THE SIAMESE TWINS, GANTER'S CAVE, 1900. Ganter's Cave was originally known as Parker's Cave and was leased to Henry Ganter by Parker for a period of 99 years in 1899. Ganter was the first to commercialize the cave after the completion of Lock & Dam #5 in 1899 and Lock #6 in 1906, which allowed boats to navigate the waters of Green River. The cave was never a commercial success and was only opened for a short period of time.

DOSSEY

DOMES

CAVERN

AND

DOSSEY CLIFF WALK.

DOSSEY DOMES CAVERN, 1912. The existence of Dossey Domes Cavern was suspected for several years after the discovery of a spring with strong air currents, but did not open until the fall of 1912. The cave was located on a hill overlooking the Green River. This is the only promotional pamphlet printed for the cave. It reads, "In the recent discovery of the Dossey Domes Cavern a march was stolen upon Nature and she was caught at her most beautiful handiwork in cave-making. It contains none of those long, rough and uninteresting avenues found in other caves, but is a revel of scenic beauty throughout." The cave was known as the "Most Beautiful of all the Caverns."

ENTRANCE TO DOSSEY DOMES CAVERN, 1912. The manager of Dossey Domes Cavern was Edmund Turner. Turner was a civil engineer who came to the Mammoth Cave area in 1912 wanting to see some caves. When he was introduced to Floyd Collins, they explored together. Turner discovered Dossey Domes Cavern in 1912, and later in 1915 he also discovered Great Onyx Cave. The wooden gate entrance to Dossey Domes Cavern is shown here.

ENTRANCE TO DIXON CAVE, 1896. It is known that Dixon Cave and Mammoth Cave are geologically the same system. The sinkhole entrance to Dixon Cave is located near the Historic Entrance to Mammoth Cave, just around the hillside. Like Mammoth Cave, Dixon Cave was mined for its saltpeter. The cave has one large continuous passageway.

Transparent Draperies,
American White Onyx Cave, Ky.
(PHOTO BY WADE H. HIGHBAUGH.)

TRANSPARENT DRAPERIES, AMERICAN WHITE ONYX CAVE, C. 1920. American White Onyx Cave was formerly known as Andy Collins' Crystal Onyx Cave, Fishback Cave, Little Beauty Cave, and Old Onyx Cave. Andy Collins was the brother of Floyd Collins. At one time, Lee Collins (Floyd's father) tried to get possession of Floyd's casket from Crystal Cave and put it near the entrance to this cave (when it was called Fishback Cave) to draw tourists.

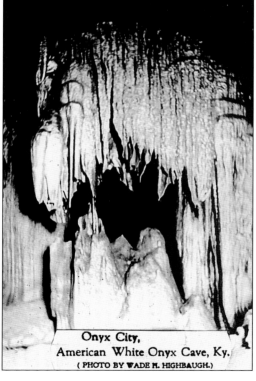

Onyx City,
American White Onyx Cave, Ky.
(PHOTO BY WADE M. HIGHBAUGH.)

ONYX CITY, C. 1920. American White Onyx was a small cave in Edmonson County. Mrs. O.H. Fishback owned the cave and the Fishback Hotel (formerly called the Mentz Hotel) during the mid-1920s. Andy Lee Collins commercially operated the cave for Mrs. Fishback. He died in 1940.

Pharaohs' Table,
American White Onyx Cave, Ky.
(PHOTO BY WADE H. HIGHBAUGH.)

PHARAOH'S TABLE, C. 1920. The entrance of the American White Onyx Cave was enlarged by dynamite to make it more easily accessible to the visitor. The cave was highly decorated with beautiful formations. Though the cave was close to the L&N Railroad, it received little visitation and was only opened for a short time. These photographs by Wade Highbaugh represent the only printed evidence of the commercial operation.

MASTODON BONES, 1928. Collins' Onyx Cave was another cave found and operated by Andy Lee Collins in 1928. As Collins was exploring this new cave, he discovered some bones close to the cave entrance. The bones were identified as that of a mastodon or mammoth.

Mastodon Bones, found at
Collin's Onyx Cave.
PHOTO BY WADE H. HIGHBAUGH.

COLLINS'
Onyx Cave

Is on the Dixie Highway, Between Cave City and Glasgow Junction

≈≈≈≈≈

IF YOU WANT TO VISIT

NATURE'S WONDERLAND

DO NOT FAIL TO SEE THIS INTERESTING SPECTACLE

≈≈≈≈≈

ON THE DIXIE HIGHWAY 4½ MILES SOUTH OF CAVE CITY, KENTUCKY

COLLINS' ONYX CAVE, 1928. Collins was co-owner of the cave with his neighbor, O.E. Turner. This was another cave that received little visitation and was only open for a short time. The photograph shows the cave's only promotional brochure, which features comments from visitors. For example, "It is with pleasure that I recommend the Onyx Cave to the public at large, the many interesting sights, which I had the opportunity of seeing, impressed me more and more, that the case truly in [sic] Nature's Wonderland. The bones of the mammal are, to say the least a very novel sight. I hereby wish to thank the management of the cave for the courtesy extended to myself and party." The brochure states that "Trips may be arranged at any hour, day or night."